“Even
After
All this time
The Sun never says to the Earth,

"You owe me."

Look
What happens
With a love like that,
It lights the whole sky.”

-Hafiz

The First Book Of Pories

The Beauty of Divine Solitude

By

Jamal McCray

The Beginning

Book One

The Beauty of Divine Solitude: The Beginning

Book Two

The Beauty of Divine Solitude: The First Trip to the Woods

Book Three

The Beauty of Divine Solitude: Purpose Birthed out of Solidarity

The Beginning

Jamal McCray
Email; Jamalmac02@hotmail.com
Instagram: J.A.Mccray
Website: www.Jamccray.com
Facebook: Jamal A. McCray

By Jamal McCray, the publisher of this work

Manufactured in the United States of America

The Beauty Of Divine Solitude: The Beginning| Jamal McCray

ISBN-13: 978-1514334065

ISBN-10:1514334062

Table of Stories

Love not the world, neither the things that are in the world. If any man love the world, the love of the Father is not in them.

For all that is in the world, the lust of the flesh, and the lust of the eyes and the pride of life, is not of the Father, but is of the world.

-1 John 2:15

Thank you Lord for this gift;
It is only right that
I give my gift back to you accordingly.

Welcome to the beginning of the wonderful imagination of Jamal A. McCray. May your travels be grand for the journey at hand.

These are some of the first stories that I wrote and this was the intro to me discovering my passion. This was a rough time in my life and I was young and naïve so to say, but all things work together for the good of those that love God; therefore my past is but a foundation to my future, as you can't build a house from the second floor first.

Enter into the world of my imagination, watch your step and lose yourself as you enter into the front door of my writings. Good day.

I Solemnly Swear

I seemingly want to float into the 17th century with no cares in the world, just me, my lady and tea time for two, while listening to Classical music and partaking of wine and cheese too.

Oh my lady how art thou, why hast thou forsaken me? Why cannot you see that my love is like an ocean? Deeper and deeper it goes, the further you delve deep into this abyss, the less you seem to know. An entire world of unimaginable beauties; I wonder if I am still talking about the Ocean, or if I am just going through the motion of waves upon its surface.

The sun no longer burns the retina of my eyes as I stare into it solemnly. I think about you and I get cold shivers that travel all throughout my body. My world is deprived without you, I run around the market place looking for bread to eat, sometimes wandering the nights looking at the sky as I walk the streets. I just sit and let the hours pass me by and I am led to a place where all I can think about is your shimmering eyes.

I think about your smile and how your hair twirls as you turn your head to look at me. I look at the present and what the past has presented for me as a gift and I displace that as my future, failing the time between you and me at this current moment. We sat in the forest and gave praise to our Lord and Savior, great revelation was poured out over unto us. Everything in the forest began to glow with a special aurora and it let us feel the magic that the trees laid before us. Everything played in sweetened perfect harmony wrapped around an autumn inspired blanket.

Can we just go back in time to the point where our minds were free and not brainwashed by the evils that were meant to be? If it weren't for Cartoon Network and Animal Planet, I probably wouldn't even watch T.V.

The Club House

Oh, well, I would like to be with you in our own little cabin located in the middle of the woods. Isolated but not too far from society with infinite drinks and movies that would seldom keep our attention. We would always stay up later than we normally should watching old movies adding side comments to the movies smiling with a grin. With a fridge that replenished all of our favorite foods. Talking about life, how it is now and how it was then.

Behind the cabin there was a path that led to a lake with a 'T' shaped dock, tied to its base was a little boat for two. It gave you that feeling like being home for the summer after school. You know when the sky is filled with the color blue and it's hot enough to melt your generic glue?

Lying in the grass as the hours went by we examined all of the flowers and the precious butterflies. Wishing that these days would last and that time never let them go by. But night time is cool that's when dark hits the sky.

"Instead can it turn into a club house? Like the ones I used to make out of sheets and chairs. On the front of the club house there would be a cardboard sign that said 'Enter if you dare', with flashlights and comic books so that we could read to each other in the dark." Think about how cool it would be to do that now with each other, in our older age. Then I begin to wonder in the end why even bother.

In a Land Far Far Away…

On the lake, ripples in my mind, thinking of things to write for you, they flow without me having to try. You and I added together is the equation of good loving and a vintage style. Surrounded by aqua as the sun creates an orange rippling effect off of the water, it reminds me of that game we used to play as children; don't touch the floor, its hot like lava.

Honey buns and drinks cover the floor of the boat. I told you that it'll warm up so you wouldn't need a coat. Let's travel so far out that we can no longer see the edge of the coast and end up on some uncharted island of our choice. There we'll build a colony out of trees and stones.. As long as you and I are on this island we shall never be alone. Just in case, I decided to bring my phone and a boom box powered by solar energy, that way we can listen to music from the eighties.

Our accessories consist of wooden objects because there are no metal ore components around us. Life is peaceful and therefore we never had reason to fuss as one another, new words we made, for when we hit our toes on camouflaged rocks and wanted to cuss, or is it curse.

Birth Of The Woods

I woke up in the middle of the forest on a warm rainy afternoon. The sun lingered in the sky but the clouds left a foggy overcast making the world around me light up. This made me think of those drawn leaf designs on my mother's tea cups. I began to walk in the midst of the forest while the rain hit the leaves softly, not getting wet. Listening to the melody created by the trees and of the rain drops, an occasional bird chirp and the passing of a small creek being blocked by a giant rock.

Tick tock, I feel like time has not changed but one thing that's different, is my mind frame. As close to a natural world as possible, you feel something speaking to you much stronger. It's a sense of belonging; beauty and a story that's rather enchanting. With good always prevailing in the end of course, so hope and faith are intertwined as one. Now rest your head while it is night and in no time be awakened by the rays of the sun. What once was a stormy night has now turned into a promising day. Forever and ever we were all simply okay.

What A Wonderfully Good Morning

Sitting by the window I looked outwards above the tree tops to see a formation of clouds shape shifting my way. How lovely this day is, is what I normally would say as I would give thanks and praise to god unlocking my minds potential, patiently going on about my way. I'll have a wonderful day full of surprises and a natural positive balance. When there are more people that are happy than there are people who are sad, everyone feels a little better but when it's vice versa everyone will be cooped at home in their cozy little shelters.

Everyone should watch the sunrise and the sun set every day, how lovely would that be. Do it for a week and you will surely start to see that you need a bit of peace, a seemingly little piece of tranquility. Maybe a little bit of Nirvana to pass the time. My favorite album is of course *Nevermind*. Let's rewind now, like your favorite part of the movie that you must memorize the lines for, while you eat hotdogs and hamburgers with ketchup that fell from out of your eyes from staring at the death box for so long. That's referring to the television just in case you missed that line.

"Now you can end the song oh tapping keys of this keyboard of mine."

The Shadows Tell Stories

Underneath of a tree I noticed three shadows as they lay before me directed by a branch being pushed by the wind. It resembles an ocean current and a whale as it sings. The grass changes before me; I'm now floating in a small sail boat humbly across the sea. Thinking how I could possibly make it out of this one, I see a bigger boat faintly in the distance. The Captain is an old short pirate, the kind with the wooden leg and an eye patch, three crew men who speak in broken English and a parrot who none the less had a French accent. Maybe finding this ship wasn't by accident or does it resemble my sub conscious thoughts hidden deep within. At least I won't be bitten by a mosquito, oh how they haunt me.

I snap back into reality and notice the second shadow. This one kind of glows, it's a planet being orbited by three moons. So I ride my skateboard down the street of this small town on this new planet and everyone is staring at me. I stare back and continue on my journey. No I'm not a small time boy living in a lonely world, although I'm in a strange land with odd clothes and no sense of direction of which way that I should be going. The fact that I don't have any friends here, I still feel popular amongst these aliens; the aliens of my mishaps and of my wrong doings. Then as I was before I'm back underneath of my tree staring out before me.

This time the sun has gone down and there are no shadows in attendance but the land before me is dark and the fields are shallow, there are fields that travel miles and miles ending up at the nearest town. Lit up by the moonlight and an occasional site of a firefly, I soon see it all as my pupils dilate and my eyes adjust. I continue to walk without a fuss, that's when I began to hear a rattle and a brush. It startled me back underneath of my tree, I guess I'll go inside now so that these mosquitoes won't get to me.

City Life

We should be together in a small little apartment in New York City learning street life and how to hustle and be witty. We'd learn to love one another's flaws and have movies such as jaws playing in the background, really not watching it so we'd decrease the sound. Listening to new music every day I say, with speakers through the apartment dancing through our daily routines, holding my nose at the smell of those sardines. We'd casually go on about our day ending it with dim lights and a book, with a cup of tea by our bed side. Telling you goodnight with a kiss on your forehead and the TV set on a 60 minute sleep period; after the two episodes of family guy goes off. 500 thread count sheets so you know the bed is soft, with retractable blinds that open up when the sunlight hits them, allowing me to see your beautiful face in a whim. Magnificent I think to myself, starting my morning off with such a beautiful sight therefore destroying all of the evils that I'd normally have to fight. See you at three, and we're off with a smile and a peace.

NATURE

Winter kills flowers and plants

And

Killing someone is always most awful

However,

The plants forgive winter

And

When the spring time comes back around

They're beautiful again

And

They've forgotten last season's winter.

Good day I said to this lovely Madame who wasn't much taller than an old wooden dresser sitting in the corner of my room. I told her I admired her unique aurora, my lunch breaks soon. Let's go on a trip; taking a walk through the woods. While holding my water bottle in which I'll soon sip, I told her I'd like to dance with her and so I grabbed her hips. I don't know, girls just like those things, especially from a misfit. Soon this became our thing, every day we'd meet by the woods and I'd read her my newest story and she'd always play a song that closely fit the mood of my worries. Right after, she'd tell me about what she thought about my mind on paper. It's like she danced to my words, I guess I'll play Good Love by Anita Baker, continuing our date passed physical barriers.

LUNAR

"You're beautiful," I told her, as I looked into her eyes by the window. While the sun began to rise, I want to live in the skies with you where'd you have no worries and no such cares. You'd just have to worry about breathing in too much air. Or we could live in a cave, like a couple of bears and hibernate from society for a couple of years but of course well preplanned. We have tons of food and electronics so that I can play sonic on Sega genesis while you watch your favorite television shows.

Holy horse poop, whenever I'm with you I go into my Zen garden, koi fish swim in the ponds underneath of the wooden bridge in the middle vicinity. It's always cloudy here and there is a heavy mist that rests upon its threshold. You don't need a jacket because it never gets that blistering cold. The mountain ranges can be seen densely through the fog, so let's sit on the edge of this log and skip rocks in hopes of scaring off some of the frogs.

That reminds me of a place where the water meets some ostentatious mass, not a place with a lot of sand but where green grass fields cover most of the land. A tree or two, some shade and an ever changing hue. The color of the world as the sun goes through its motions. Light over here, dark over there but I think the shade is just the nighttime hiding, scared of the sun so it hides behind things so that the sun can't reach it, so that the sun can't impeach it.

What's next is not up to us; let us hurry down these trails without a fuss, but in a rush, passing flowers and plants that can't grow around people. It's so peaceful and yet so intricately hidden. I'll pick you some and make you a bouquet of flowers to show you that I think about you each and every hour. Add some flour and we have a dinner by the woods, playing instruments that make all of the little forest creatures dance. Taking their stance, I thought they were only in stories but when they played their instruments the fire it began to rumble. It rumbled and rumbled until you could see art made with the flares of the flames. Oh man I thought that this was insane, until I fell asleep and was woken up at about five a.m. by the moon whispering in my left ear, it told me of a romance between the ocean and itself and how the sun always seems to snatch it back in the oncoming hours. I could see that the moon was quite devastatingly sad and so I agreed to help. But the moon continued to stay angry and it soon began to pout. I told it to grow up, you are so very much older than I, so we just laughed it off and the moon continued to shine in the skies.

Moonlight Sonata

By the time you arrived it was rainy and the ground was dry. The earth had given up on itself and so it began to cry. The trees were gone and the grass had died. All that was left was the moon and the sky.

This was the beginning of a new era of life, driven by love and moon light. The days weren't sunny it was more of a bright white. Rivers overflowed the land, only high ground was suitable for livelihood. This time around everything was flowing backwards; the ocean, the sea's, everything in between. A world with no sun, what have we done? To adapt to moonlight would be a challenging feat.

The days were as long as about two weeks. No day, no night, just a glimmer of light from the moon every 27 hours. It was still always dark and so lights were plastered up in every corner. We made it work and we are still working at it today. The constant moon rays turned the grass a light purplish color. Trees glistened now as if they were coated with diamond paint. Maybe we survived because everyone was as peaceful as saints. We just lived in this new beautiful world and always gave thanks.

Adventure Awaits

Fight the long fight young lad, grab your horse and gather three bags. We'll need it for this long journey we are about to trek. I'm still telling everybody that my captain was Kirk. But despite working long hours, every hour not working is thus much better. I'll write you a blueberry letter and tell you of my adventures. The adventures that shape our life, the ones that lay out our personality. Who are you and is that who you want to be? All adventures come to an end though, and then I'll tell you everything in which I've learned; when I was stubborn and still unborn. Until I had a revolution of the mind that makes you wonder about the goodness of life instead of the struggles in this world that make you want to eventually stop trying. Stories that if you listen to and take heed, your life will drastically become better. It's like cheat codes for life in the form of knowledge. Now step back off the ledge my friend and let's fly instead but hold on one second, I forgot to eat breakfast and I have yet to make up my bed. Of course, the Adventure really begins when you meet Jesus, for He did not come to make bad people good but to give dead people life. Now reread the story one more time.

Morning Drives

Driving down the road early in the morning while a pink haste sets the mood, I am just another soul living life through a daily commute in this forsaken world trying only to experience things that will fill me with joy. None the less everything will still unfurl. The sun has not risen completely it still has crest in its eyes. You can see the rays of the sun trying to make their way in between the clouds in the sky. Technically riding in a car you're levitating a couple feet above the ground, but that's another story like does a tree make a sound, if no one is around to hear it. What if you feel it instead and it sent sound waves through your head while you were sleeping soundly in your bed. While you're sleep you don't have to worry about anything. You can have dreams like being in a world made of sand where we always held hands or an earth where we lived in the sky and the ground was above us. I don't really understand what all the fuss is, some things are bad but there are a lot more things in this world that would offer you tokens of good rather than sacrifices of sad. Watch Alice in wonderland, learn about the mad hatter, sit underneath a tree or grab a ladder, so that you can spray paint graffiti in unknown locations leaving your mark upon the world. Just don't say that I told you to do so.

Waltz If I May

As the song was playing all I could think about was she and I dancing, waltzing if you may. All that mattered to me was her beautiful face looking up to me as we danced gracefully across the floor. Everyone stood around us watching us dance, it was something like a moving art form at most.

Pachelbel Canon in D Minor was playing and you were wearing this stunningly beautiful dress, it was tan, at the end of the sleeves it grew thin and turned into lace linen. Around the waist it began to get poufy and it made you look like a tent, looking beautiful as ever. As the song began to pick up others joined in and we all danced gracefully across the wooden floor. Not a step out of sync, classical 17th century dancing at its finest. Outside there was a beautiful field where the sun sat in the horizon. Beautiful flowers and bushes outlined the field, a pathway that you and I dared to follow. You let go of my hand, we split our ways. We ran around this elegant maze and ended up running into each other once again.

At this point in time we just walk circles around each other. Our eyes never leaving the others sight; shall we dance one more dance of unforgettable pleasure.

I pull you in close then release you back into the grassy wonderland. Only to pull you back into my romantic entanglement. Is this how our love is meant to be? You always leaving me and then returning at the moment of almost no return?

Dusty Old Attic

I have this summer time move to a new neighborhood crush on you. As if we would go on tons of adventures like exploring the woods and sneaking into the old lady's house when she went away on her grocery trips. We got in through the garage; we went up the steps and scavenged through the cupboards of her dusty old attic. Noticing her old school TV with a rotating turning knob, I could only think about the static. Little Black and white dots hypnotizing your mind like a zebra who's too hard to find. Never mind, let's just get out of here and explore another part of this town. Like the old burger joint down the street. A potential story spot that we'd tell our kids about how we first met and how we used to go down to the bay and get our feet wet. Two people in love and yet unforeseen circumstances must drive us apart. Love should have no boundaries, it should be above all things, but you must not lose your mind; you must stay happy and sing. Sing a song about three little birdies telling you about the sun and their views from the tree tops above. So as we become two instead of one I'll remember our stories and our deep affectionate love. I won't depart with hate in my heart instead I'll release my clasped hands and out of them will fly a dove.

It is now turning dusk and we smell like burger meat or whatever smells make you do a little jig and gallop your feet. Let us go to the park it should be empty now. I know a little spot even though I live on the other side of town. I call it Woodstock because it's through a trail behind the park. The journey takes us past wild growing flowers and different color tree bark, way past any pavement being drawn on with street chalk from little kids who can barely walk or talk. It's sheltered by trees as if they were covering a dream; I discovered it one day while exploring, walking alongside the stream.

I just knew I'd have to bring somebody here because it appeared to be too good as it seemed. And you know how that goes it usually is. Give me a second though, I just need to take a whiz, I'll get back to you shortly so we can get down to business. It could be the past it could be the future I just know I had an old handheld TV I took from the old ladies house and it had a great picture. So we watched some TV as the night passed us by. Staring at the milky way as it hung over us in the sky, pointing out other constellations. I really, really want some potatoes maybe a hamburger; hold the tomatoes. Maybe I don't know what I want; I just want to want nothing with you at this very exact moment.

Oh Dear

Dusk is kind of awesome it's the setting when you first fall in love, in some summer in the 90's. Where we used to swing on the hammock and play paperboy on our game consoles, you always brought joy to my soul but that's the past; let's move on to the future where we'll travel the globe calling every new place home. From the grasslands, to New Zealand's elephant rocks, I just wanted to tell you that you rock both pair of my socks. I wear two pairs because it's more comfortable. Don't forget that I need my graduation socks to match my stole.

What kind of chemistry do you have to have when you make music with someone? It's rather interesting to say the least. Making music at one point and then being able to make a perfect grilled cheese. I like the dance you did after you ate your grilled cheese; you jumped up, turned side to side and grabbed one knee. Then you sung I believe I can fly, a tear drop fell down my left eye. It was a resemblance to the blue in the sky, around 8:49. A quarter after nine and I'll pour us some more wine, like the kind a waiter would bring us at a fancy dine in some Paris restaurant; oh what a lovely town.

Free Man

I sit and think and tote and sink, into my chair listening to California dreaming. Wishing I had some sinsemillia, but for right now I'll chill in the back of my mind and see the connections in the world happening right before me. Looking out the window as it begins to rain. Wouldn't it be nice to go outside and play in and have not one drop of rain touch me. Dry in the midst of a wet shower, like being different such as Booker T. Washington in the reign of Dwight Eisenhower. In a setting where it was always cloudy and the skies were grey. The roads were dirt paths someday hoping to be turned into sediment rock that we drive our cars on today. Nature is everywhere so the clouds move faster, it might rain so I'll sit in the middle of a field and watch the thunderous disaster. I'll walk the paths laid before me by previous passersby, hoping to run into someone. I'll trade them wine for honey, or I'll sell them my famous tea for money. Maybe I'll sell enough to buy a horse; I'll call her Lola bunny. Ironic because it's a horse why is it called a bunny. Why do you do things that you know are wrong, same principle different circumstance, still walking listening to Justice.

Just do the DANCE, while you pull up your pants and grab your headphones because a tree branch pulled it out. It tried to grab a listen. Just for that, I'll turn it into maple syrup and sit it in my kitchen, pour it on my pancakes made from wheat I grew for about six weeks. Thanks to these oncoming downpours, the greenery will be fed for days to come. How come the Indians didn't have problems when they tried to grow their crops, but now we have chemicals and pesticides that kill our insides? But you know, I'll just continue walking down this path. Hoping, wishing, I'll do something extravagant one day, that brings joy to others and money to those that surround me. Plan goals and set them into motion when the time is right, but for now fall back on the grass and let the rain hit you while the UV rays shine bright.

Fishing

Chilling by the dock, it's about 7 O'clock. The beautiful sunset mixes in with the clouds reflecting on the bay. The clouds in the distance foreshadow the night after the day. The fishes are biting like crazy but we're just chilling, you know relaxing acting lazy. My friend with his girl, it's like a mini vacation; there's a gentle breeze, the waves vibrate in the direction. Feet hanging off the dock, now look up notice the trees from afar, Oh I got a tug; just caught a small fish, where's the jar? Night's coming slowly and coming faster, the breeze is picking up, getting stronger, longer lasting.

Quiet storm in the evening this day turned into something meaningful. There's a factory in the background, it's kind of ironic, me sitting here relaxing and the worlds being polluted each and every summer. Days like these you can't take for granted, it's the small things in life that keeps us united. No drama, I'm getting sleepy just wake me up tomorrow.

Fire Worked

Instead of holding in your anger for some past arrangement I'll write about life and in a second it'll be the reverse feeling of flight or fight when I'm in danger. I'll tell you good stories of things to come, which will sadly involve feeling like a bum, just take some time and sit on your bum. Look out the window and stop watching TV; watch a leaf fall down from a tree. Kick a rock with the front of your toes, walk through the woods and let go of all of your woes. You aren't meant to hold these things in. They'll manifest and grow into a personality or worse a sin. Then no longer will drinking a sweet tea down by the river be exciting because you'll lose focus of the natural balance. Feelings of happiness derived from your imagination. It's that simple and yet so hard to do. Being upset is an illusion. If you can get upset in a second why can't you do the same for happiness and so I'll tell you things that'll help and fix your pants with some love and a belt. A kiss on the cheek and the feeling of winning the Olympics five times like Micheal Phelps but right now let me just embrace your presence with some classical music and the TV on low, creating a bit of light; a glow, so that I may continue to flow onwards towards mine and your growth. Into righteous beings with low lit egos, just two kids living in America where the Nations animal happens to be the Bald Eagle.

Ee.Tea.

I woke up in a strange place, where the whole economic system wasn't a rat race. The grass was brown and made little whistling sounds but it kind of levitated an inch above the ground. Almost like a mist that would determine if the day would be hot or not. A judge of water particles that sentences the sun to shine down on the planet and feed it UV rays. The land was very huge in mass, every few minutes you would notice a horse eating a bushel of hay. No one had cars everyone walked with guitars on their backs, they were long haired hippies and afro blacks. The thought of driving a luxury automobile such as a Cadillac wasn't thought of, the motive wasn't for self gain, it was more like a utilitarianism type of society; Everyone doing things for the better good of humanity. Somehow playing music and talking about ideas kept everyone's sanity. They would form circles around a fire and dance with the serenity creating a new type of tranquility that you couldn't help but be dragged into the atmospheric feeling that was presented. Manifesto there was no chipotle. There was no McDonald's or Burger King. Everyone was already intelligent and so the school system couldn't really teach them anything. Like the ancient Egyptians they sought out knowledge through reasoning of the world. Staring at the stars at night in order to determine how much potential light would shine on the world the next day. Waking up in vast fields filled with sustainable foods, no one had homes, we lived like those short statues in old ladies yards; gnomes. I guess I have to go back to earth, so like an extra terrestrial that was famous back in the day it is now my time to phone home.

Suburbs

As I listened to my favorite playlist while staring out of the passenger side window, I watched the passing trees and the occasional speeding car who completely disregards the safety of others in the same vicinity. We passed mountains and old farmer's houses with rows of corn stalks conquering their lands. A McDonald's once every 30 miles, cows and horses living seemingly harmless on luscious green hills; a house being powered by a couple of huge windmills. The grass hasn't been cut in a while so there's a couple of daisies and weeds that give the land a sense of community. Continuously traveling and now there's nothing but land, that travels further east, further west, should I go on to say the rest? A couple of satellite towers at the peak of the mountains to achieve the best cell phone reception per hour. See in the mountains there was just clean air and peace, everyone was nice and there was no greed. Why can't everyone just stay like that in their daily lives? "Peace," I said as the mountains now trailed my back and my feelings started to fade the further I got away from my peaceful meditation back into this clustered community of perpetual motion. What's the commotion, I promise you my life will be filled with peace even if I have to just pack my bags and leave. As I roll down my sleeves and tie my shoes real right. You know what, I just might.

Ance(Stor-y)

Would you listen to me if I told you the history of a group of people slowly fading from the universe? People who think outside of the circle, dislikes the color purple and used to watch family matters in the 90's and still try to imitate Urkle. But just like the grass that turns tan like hay once it's being burned by the sun, add a little water and it'll be green in no time. That's when the ants will form a single filled line. Back into their dirt mounds that go down to the earth an infinite number of times. Okay-okay what does ants have to do with anything but what does anything have to do with anything?

Why can't I just imagine a world made out of wood or cardboard or maybe even water? Wouldn't that be neat? Please-please make yourself at home, take a seat. I'll finish the story in a second.

At that moment I forgot about my story and all I could do was look at her in her perfection laid upon my bed. Trying not to act like a sucker it was soon starting to affect me. I got us some movies from the red box, care to watch? I'll play the movie and never hit stop, then I'll drop the remote off the bed creating a thump.

Once the remote falls no one wants to get it. Especially when you're plump right on the bed and the movie is getting to the climax, but lord knows I wasn't paying attention to it. I wasn't worried about tomorrow or how I was going to make three stacks. I was more interested in words flowing out of your mouth into the atmosphere making my mind form images and scenes that we both could play in. Like a couple of kids held back an extra 10 minutes from recess because I passed you a note in class and got caught. Continuing the scenes until we're both just lying there in total serene. I like you; I mean, I love you but the scene has to end, just like a dream.

Stuck in between like an old pair of jeans, lying down next to the remote on my imaginary floor, on the deck of a boat, in its pool, on an imaginary float, in the middle of winter with a big ole coat, trying to find some grass like I was a goat. Losing all faith in humanity but still I harvest my hope.

Toilet Thoughts

I wonder what life must be like to be known as GREAT and when it was first known. Maybe it was known when you were flown into the heavens or was it when you were in the deep blues of sea which will make you see there is so much life on the planet that, it would take an eternal lifetime to understand it. Collecting knowledge instead of going to college what a bum this scum of the earth has birthed. Barely scratching the surface of where he wants to be in life praying everyday he doesn't end up in a hearse because of this curse. Because birthed an African young man with no plan, father shot and killed in the desert sand. Getting to know thyself amongst the land, as well as trying to become a better man. Fame wasn't in his plan, but his father left a note saying be great son do the best you can. If you fail to plan you plan to fail said the wise fox that was trapped in a box. Got caught up by the distractions in life and every action has a reaction. Action was this fox getting caught in the box reaction, spreading the knowledge, go to college get a great job! Work for the system and get pissed on. Nah! I'll go far maybe to Mars perhaps I'll take the car and make it safely with no scars.

By Suber

NONCHALANT

Puff the magic dragon, my pants I just pulled up so they are no longer sagging. This beautiful girl, I just passed her so I turned around and looked at her as I proceeded to ask "do you like dancing in open fields under the stars, making a campfire and roasting smorz?" I hope my words weren't starting to bore. The way I would kiss her I already started to adore. Mrs. Frizzle showed me your anatomy I admire your face and our spirituality. I got her number and now I just looked at her. I'll text you eventually, but it's not like it mattered.

I can relate

Hello world, hello future, hello new things I've yet to discover. Hello girl, over there in her own little world. Thinking all of this as I ride my back around the park, wondering where my mind went in this space and time, contempt.

Watching birds fly towards some destination in the sky, where will they go, no one knows but that's the beauty in it I suppose. I also suppose that the sky goes from dusk to dawn with no in-betweens, just me, you, a blanket, some vegetables and a movie that pushes us because we are as you could say intellectuals brought down in order to make an understanding of the world for those who can't see the beauty in a tree that has no squirrels. And yet they all go through cycles, they die and come back to life again, what if we could do that. I'd really be 1000 years old but we die in other ways. Don't worry this is just a phase.

The journey has yet to begin. I was listening to this song called a horse with no name. It's very clever you see it's about a desert. Traveling on a horse with no origins, I hope this has yet to be boring. In the desert the sun peaks over the horizon and turns your skin red. Your only goal is to follow the live stock to the nearest river bed. Maybe you can drink some water maybe you can't. It's worth a try.

Once you're done you have many miles left to travel, down mountain valleys and dry rivers. At night the temperature drops so it'll make you shiver. So you'll want to sit down pull out a spliff and sing a Bob song to make the time vortex shift. There's a natural mystic in the air making you high off of your own understanding of the world. If you want to get higher you have to understand more. Your receptors must be open by eight or your employees in this case THC will be late. But forget that, keep smoking in this hot oasis called the desert. Cutting many a cactus open in hopes of finding some water. Mirages in the distance keep you from going insane, like a goal in life to fool your brain. That's it I give up, getting out of the desert seems a task that's almost impossible, like living in the middle of the Pacific Ocean with no boat. That's when I saw it; I saw puff, that's the magical dragon of the west coast

I Have To Be At Work In 5

There's this mystical land that I go to in my head, it's like Narnia for the brain. You just close your eyes and think about a land full of amazement and wonder, a land full of surprises, where things that you once knew are but a mere drop of water within the ocean. Have you ever run through the woods at dusk with only the moonlight guiding your path? All you can see is my shadowy figure dashing through the trees. Do you want to kiss in the middle of the forest in an enchanted land?

The trees whisper great nothings in your ear as the butterflies float up towards the sky and turn into stars. The trees gently sway back and forth to keep us cool on the hot summer night. I think it's time to call it a night, these woods host a lot of creatures. The sunrise will wake us up literally. The morning sun glistens as it reflects off of the dew on the ground. What started off as a damp morning turns into a dry early afternoon. Flowers and pedals are being gently pushed through the wind. The trees step aside as we walk through its depths creating a path that we must follow, what awaits us at the end of the path, we won't know until we get there. But we must make this journey, together, on an epic quest. Then I open my eyes and it's time for work. Be back later mind.

Superfast Horses

I'm listening to *Undun,* that's a song, while writing, oh fun. Drinking fruit punch and eating cinnamon grahams. Across the world people are fighting for Uncle Sam. Writing notes to you in between my call of duty games. Staring out the window looking at the rain, I just think about you in some sort of happy marshmallow land. "You dress so odd little boy," she said as I pretended to listen.

With my headphones in I was listening to music as everything began to glisten. We traveled across the land at night on a magic flying horse. Across rivers and land masses that you'd only see on the back of a postcard. Can we land down there by the big elephant rock? Is it warm enough to go to sleep without our socks? I don't know so we just laughed and fell gracefully on our backs, stared up at the stars and begin to remember all that we had.

How we could build a partnership that would last to the end of time, a rhyme that would be better than all other rhymes. So let's begin there's no time. Dancing to the sounds of fishes jumping out of the water, I wanted to go for a swim; do you think we ought to? Have you ever sat around and listened to a melody on an ocarina? You ever played Final Fantasy and summoned the ice queen Shiva? You ever wrote a story while walking in the rain, with no cares in the world because it's all the same? And then I arose in our marshmallow land. My feelings were then so dense and deadly like 10 square feet of quick sand. I began to grab the sides of my head with my hands, hoping that I would find new plans in this marshmallow land.

Social Crisis

Can't you see the planet mercury? My spaceship has landed, what exactly is my destiny? No more traveling through the dark abyss of space, wondering where I'd stop even though I don't know this place. It's funny how love can be compared to space and how the shape of your heart can take the formation of a face. How, dancing through grasslands during the middle of the day could leave lasting memories that would always stay.

Tall dandelions and wheat's, they're tall enough to come up to my sleeves. Even the grass is tall enough to reach my knees. Let's climb a tree, make a club house and start a colony. There is an emotion that is intertwined between you and me; it consists of four letters, no not love but care. Because you care about your friends and they seem to last substantially longer than three weeks like some people's weddings. Let's make new memories, it snowed today let's go sledding, then buy a dog and brush him whilst it is shedding. I just want a little tender love like Otis Redding. How come listening to Mozart provokes such strong feelings. Like the trees talking or a house with a glass ceiling. The moon battles asteroids to protect the Earth. However humans are destroying it from the inside out. Cutting down trees and killing cows, making 50 page magazines to check out the next new styles. A McDonald's every corner, three in every mile, wow. Just drew a circle on my wall with some magic chalk that takes me to a new place, like jack and the bean stalk. Don't sit around let's explore let's walk. Open your mind, don't be quiet let's talk. Look over there not too far from here is a park, let's walk fast it is beginning to become dark. I feel the same dangers as being in a tub with a shark. However I'm with you which meant that we are together not apart. Now I must go, don't miss me it is life. There's no need to fight. There's magic where I'm going. You are as powerful as your mind. Open a book; take a magic carpet ride. I can show you the world or we can just stay inside.

THE BACK OF THE HOUSE; THE FRONT OF THE HOUSE

Writing makes me feel high, not the kind of high from smoking on a dime. But the kind of high that makes me feel enlightened with the skies, a sense of one with the world, all underneath the power of my control.

I have this shed that I'd like to camp in with you on a warm summers night. When the winds are low and the moon shines bright. The moonlight makes the inside of the shed light up because of the many cracks, shimmering off of the dew on the grass. Making you glow like a flashlight behind a pane of glass. I enjoy your company you have a very elegant sense of class. The shed is a cold place though, there's only one exit and there are no windows. So please don't pass the gas because whoever smelt it dealt it, which is pretty much the bimbo.

My friends keep lookout on top of the trees above us. Just in case other strongholds try to conquer us. I truly don't know what all of the fuss is. Let's stay uncivilized and live off of knowing that iron things will began to rust, instead of coming up with a solution to reverse the process. How rude of me, you have on such a lovely dress, I'm sure you'd win all types of contests. Just watch out for the step by the door. Someday I'll finish nailing it to the floor. So hopefully you won't trip, hit your head and end up acting like those kids off of jersey shore. Speaking of such, I think I want to make some smorz, time to go on a quest and discover what my backyard has in store. Let us begin.

Off into this vast wonderland we go, across tall grasslands where beautiful trees can be seen faintly in the distance. The more you walk to them the more they seem like a mirage and yet in an instant. All of nature put together somehow makes a natural collage. But really it's just night time in my backyard, crossing brick paths, not stepping in between them, avoiding the grass because it is lava and if your feet touches it, you'd be sent back home to your momma. She'd be sad and then go on a vengeance raid to all of the other escapades that'll take place in this forsaken land. The trees will bleed and lose their leaves; I'll rake them up and listen to Creep, that's a Radiohead song that makes you think. Makes you find a rock and toss it into the street, while taping your foot till this ill rotten beat.

Making new constitutions so that we can control our land and yet at the end of the day we just threw it away. Forget these rules, let all of us rule. Let's go to town hall and spray paint it brown. After we leave town hall we'll travel back to the wilderness to find new shelter that we need before it begins to thunder.

You're much more fun than I expected, I couldn't have picked a better selection. The trees send us messages in a secret language. It takes us ten hours just to decipher three pages. Sitting Indian style now in some unknown location, the moon is no longer in the middle of the night sky; it's sitting sideways like the boys back in the day. The moon is now beginning to close its eyes. That is when the morning dew will start to glisten with the littlest bit of sunlight. Leaving wet footprints as we step onto the cold pavement barefoot. That'll eventually dry as I'm waving goodbye. It's time to part ways because I don't know what else to say. I'm trying to be cool while refraining from being a fool. Once in the shed, we fled to the backyard, now we're heading east towards the new world, which is really the front yard.

By the time we got to the front yard it was beginning to become morning. Staying up all night we were really bored then. Without any supplies and a lack of oxygen, I'll look at the videos from Coachella and go to the store and grab a jar of Nutella. Put it on my bread and watch you act a fool as you sing under my umbrella. I guess I'll go hunt in the woods so that we could have some feedback from our harvest. Like the Beatles said I am the Walrus. I am the moon man traveling through space and time on a journey destined through the benign to stop all of the evils that will rise up in this world, so that the future may be bright for all of the beautiful girls. Then one day I'll be able to sit on the stoop in front of my house, spit in a bucket and smoke something exquisite. Rocking in my chair with overalls on, in the middle of nowhere like courage the cowardly dog. With a boom box that plays cassette tapes, with some old air Jordan five grapes. With my lady who also likes to escape, likes to go to random places and just lay. Like a hippie in this modern day or era. Who is not a hipster and hates the idea of putting on mascara. What's next after we leave the front yard? I don't drink so I'll never be at the bar, forget a happy hour. You should be happy all the time. This is the end and so we go inside the front door one more time.

Reminiscing

I'm blasting The Roots, sitting down tapping my foot. I started thinking about everything in such a good light, like making up with your friends after a huge fight or driving in the rain underneath of the orange street lights. In elementary school learning to play three blind mice, trying to impress this girl I thought looked nice. Wanting Air Jordan's because I thought they'd help me take flight. Staying up on Saturdays to watch Snick at Night. Playing tag; I have to be home before the street lights.

Little daredevil, never was scared of heights, never had the chance to fly a kite. However I use to play paperboy with this girl I used to like. Sitting on a hammock, I began to mimic her just because I knew it would bring happiness to her world.

My granddad met my grandma at nine, that's a match made in heaven back then. Too bad this world is too full of sin; too many people want to do the wrong thing. They should have watched Spike lee's movie *Do The Right Thing*, instead of *Boy'z in the hood* and instead began their greed for bling. Admire everything for what it's worth, cause sooner than later we'll all be in the back of a hearse, can I wipe off that smile, not in a bad way, in a way that makes you cry like after having your first child.

My father won best dressed in high school I guess that's where I got my style. Fannie Mae foundation yeah

I walked the five miles. When I was little I hated the music from the X-Files. Clothes on my floor lay in piles, lying on my back I'm dreaming about visiting the Nile. Going to Egypt to visit the pyramids, but right now I am in Maryland instead. So make my day.

Natures Economy

Let's eat brownies, listen to champagne supernova and dance crazily in the woods. On a blanket of leaves, a roof top made of trees and a protective agency service known as bees.

Home grown remedies keep us from falling ill to the dangers of the wilderness, contempt with the fact that we just need to be closer to nature and not manmade sky scrapers or structures. No technology, which means no social inactivity. When you create a ship you also create the shipwreck. Please understand that I don't need the manifestation of interactivity in order to sufficiently feel a particular way about you. I can hold my feelings high above me like apple's new program cloud. Recall them when needed and then my problem is treated.

Soft spoken by your words I'd like to show you mine's next. Maybe it'll leave a lasting impression and tomorrow morning you and I could be at Ihop eating breakfast. Talking about life stories, then what's next? If you really think you have game, you have not played me yet.

Something Short, Something Neat.

Just waking up in the early morning I give thanks to God, I don't know but today seems pretty odd. Hectic static on my television, I can't watch my morning cartoons. So I'll go back to bed and take a nap until the crack of noon. Then I'll wake up and be like oh snap I forgot about school, and write my teacher an email and say "oh I was a fool." Listening to stairway to heaven the entire time, scrolling through my phone writing down lines that describe what I'm doing in a way unimaginable. If you want your kids to be intelligent read them fairy tales. Imagination is the cause of everything because if you can't think about a thing it can't come to pass.

Do I really Have To Wake Up For Work?

I really enjoy the morning, waking up early stretching your arms out and yawning. Dawn is like the perfect setting for anything that you may want to do. Like sitting in my car having a picnic with food or listening to my favorite playlist because it just fits every mood; Waking up at five and standing in the middle of the woods.

I just think it's something that we could do, instead of watching movies and relaxing like we're used to. There's a certain smell that lingers in the air like the world is waking up, looking out of their windows just to stare. Like my friend on that cold spring night. Birds are communicating through tweets and chirps. My nephew is eating breakfast as he begins to burp. When you look at things do you see the beauty in them or do you just see it for what it is. I live my life like these writings putting such complex thoughts into such delicate objects.

Morning time means all of the commuters are riding the metro underground. Up above you can't hear a sound. I guess when they arrive at their destination they'll be glad that they made it safe and sound. Next they'll give everyone they know daps and pounds, then after work head back in to the east side town. The town is a village like medieval times. Drawing pictures and painting using Fibonacci spiral lines, jousting with horses in order to practice against the evil forces. You know the goblins and ghouls that terrorize the neighborhoods but other than that it's just an average morning.

AMERICA

I was sitting on the ranch chewing on an oak tree branch. On top of the old wooden fence, watching the horses prance and dance a dance that puts them in a trance. I'll hop off of this fence someday and pull up my pants. This is when I'll start my journey to the Netherlands outside of the ranch. I heard people over there have tons of things to do. They have the internet and they seem to lack dignity and respect. Some parents even take the coward route and choose to neglect. Some people have more money than most and some people have no money at all but it's okay, they're okay with poor people struggling as long as they're safe at home cuddling the night away by a fire place, headed to a fiery place. Although I hear the thrift stores are nice, and these lovely animals haunt people called mice. They're not so bad though, they're welcomed here.

The only thing that we have to fear is a coyote trying to attack our chicken stoop. Like an eagle piercing down with a sudden swoop. On the ranch we grow and cook our food, over there I hear they have shops where they process their food. Oh my, my insides already want to blow up inside. Hospitality is served if someone passes by and yet I've heard stories over there where people wouldn't even help someone even if they were about to die.

I don't know maybe I don't want to leave, I enjoy the horizon of the mountains outlining the bottom of the sky and the trees as they wave in the wind as I walk on by. I would miss the water as it splish and it splashes with salmon swimming upstream being caught by a bear. Wait, yeah I'll stay right here.

A Small Adventurer

I stepped on a leaf and I heard it crunch, overlooking the little line of ants bringing food to the queen because she needs her lunch. Adventure Time! I said to my little lad companion. Who has been with me since I first became the champion. We fought ghouls and giant rats, hill giants and screeching bats.

After we were done adventuring we would eat until we were fat. We would sit outside and stargaze into outer space hoping one day we'd see another race. We would just count the stars knowing we'd never finish but it always gave us a reason to do it again.

I Can't Eat Another Chicken Box

Sitting in the cafe, I'm up so I'll write fast. In this disastrous catastrophe I'll reminisce of days when I packed my laptop and walked counterclockwise up the street, listening to crazy rhythms and raps behind instruments and sick twisted beats. One thing I learned was that the seconds go by then weeks and weeks. Time goes faster as your age climbs the ladder. Crushing up and rolling up soon comes to a halting stop, baffling you to understand that it was all a trap. What's wrong with toting papers, smoking and inhaling, enticing all these pretty girls to join in on our reindeer games, flying highly, still keeping in mind that the world is one and your problems are creations from a world made for someone else? A book is a gateway, and a shelf is still just a shelf. Just remember to keep notice on the status of your health because eventually it'll be all you have left in order to live a productive life. Living a productive life and I'll emit positive energy focused on a wife. Somewhere over the rainbow skittles will drop and the stereotype of a sambo will disappear like my breakfast after not eating for three days, locked in a cell with no service for my cell phone to make an outgoing call to someone in Arabia also named Jamal.

Short Mind Work

You thought I was going to say something else, how could I pass up the chance to digress and listen to Pachelbel Canon in D minor, my favorite Classical song. As I continue to write my stories as if they were songs from a place far-far away. Let's travel to England and travel down paths on horseback, during the middle of the evening. It's becoming fall now so we need a small jacket. You look cute, like a baby llama. You're supposed to treat girls like you would treat your mama.

Moonlight sonata, how I wish I could sit on the crescent of the moon and read a book to the earth and witness the rebirth of minds everywhere. Some still swear, some don't care but I'm not trying to take it there. Let's go back to my place in the midst of the air. Like leaving the fair with the girl you love, always giving thanks to the man up above. Peace.

The Autumn Shed Of Love

Sitting on the edge of my bed, Indian style, I'm in a leafy shed. White clouds and orange leaves with a grass stain on my favorite pair of jeans. I sit and think, as to what time will bring. As I listen to the earth sing a beautiful melody. I float down the river on a small little boat with you by my side, with a gentle breeze and your light brown eyes. The breeze has picked up and if you start to shiver I shall keep you warm, through the rainy weather and cold dark storms. My feelings for you aren't the norm; let's watch a movie in my dorm. Then later on we can eat canned corn.

Your love and affection is what I yearn for, passing by these beautiful burgundy, green and orange backdrops I hope the car ride never stops. The journey is usually the best part. "*You can't hide love*" as earth wind and fire plays in the background. The music is so loud but I can still hear the sounds of your heart beat. The sound that makes me oh so weak; I need to see you more than twice a week.

Whenever we hangout I can't help this smile that comes upon my cheeks. I get nervous around you as if I had a big speech. I think I'm big meech, I have my hood up and I'm just staring into space, no I'm not a creep. I just like to think. I like to believe that this was meant to be, I like to believe that life can began with you and me. I saw a sign that said all of this because two people fell in love. Then I began to think about doves, then I began to foreshadow my life from up above.

As I sat there you hit me with a light saber, I'm turning into captain save them but I can't save you when I needed saving myself, both of us out in the water, I'm running out of breath. What to do when you are by yourself and you know you'd rather be with someone else? The sky is the limit but the roads go the distance.

Bicycle & A Pond

I'm just riding my bike through the neighborhood enjoying life, letting the breeze pass me by. Pedaling onwards I'm feeling high, passing people sitting on their porches, on an old vintage bike with a metal basket in the front. It's hot right now because we are now in the stages of a warm front. I just want to go on for days down a never ending hill learning new knowledge equivalent to the story of Jack and Jill. I notice a lightning bug every once in a while if I'm lucky enough to catch it in my peripheral vision. Still pedaling you would think that I was on a specific mission but no.

I just wish more people would listen. Somehow, sometime in my life I began to notice the beauty in everything around me. Stories much deeper than black ink on paper read by a kindergarten teacher, somehow shaping my mind at an early age so that I could transform your thoughts into images that appear to be real life.

So I'll take a right at this entrance, it leads to the pond, the one where we'll sit and recite our rhymes. The pond is full of pollen so it resembles the color of lime. When the sun reflects on its surface it's a mixture of a lemon color as well. So I guess we have a compound material called sprite. Mix it in with the moon and you have a clear contraption. That'll keep your thoughts open until the next day's satisfaction. But for right now I'll just keep on riding.

The Beginning And The End

Let's sit and think about things while cello concerto in E minor plays in the background carelessly. Let our thoughts form images above our heads, creating stories that we may jump into at any point in time. I prefer if it's after nine. I love you but let's chill instead, let's dream and dream and lay in bed. Breaking rules because it feels better instead.

Standing in time out as a kid pulling the paint off the walls, wondering why I was so bad and why I liked the season fall. Writing about the images I remember from South Carolina, woods and tree's and deer's and bee's. This magic moment, why don't you sing along with me? And yet I'm happy now in my balcony overlooking it all, enjoying new ideas walking slowly down this hall.

Will it ever end I do not know. But the show, the show it must go on. It must continue but we must prolong. As we move in slow motion to another classical song. Sitting Indian style with other kids watching hermit the frog, this crap is fake turn it off turn it off. Don't pass me that nasty eggnog. The song from little bear is called cello suite number 1 in G minor but instead I'll listen to the sugarplum fairy. I prefer the flavor cherry, banana is a no go, kind of like go-go. Let us walk slowly into the woods now like it was meant to happen but are things really meant to happen or are they by chance, Isn't that kind of the same thing. That's kind of like philosophy.

Why'd you sit next to me? Did your mind tell you to? The ocean is only blue because it is the less absorbed pigment. Why are you looking at me so, we've only gone so far in the woods where our shadows must go. The trees block the sun and all we can hear is the gentle hum of the breeze, going in-between our knees. The trees are swaying as began to fall, the leaves. I began to unroll my sleeves because there is a greater breeze. Check the steeze; I thought someone was with me. I see the lamppost maybe the wardrobe is nearby maybe I'll finally live in the sky instead of on earth where we will all eventually die. I'm on top of the world. It all depends on how you see yourself through thy own eyes. There are a lot of lows but you can't have lows without the highs and you can't live life without asking why. Why am I writing when I'd rather have someone next to me, but its okay I'll just watch Family Guy and write like I'm used too.

Sheer Coincidence

I called her on the phone and it rang and it rang and it rang; she called back and it rang and it rang and it rang. Singing along to the theme song of Malcolm in the middle "You're not the boss of me now," pass along this way we need more tree's now. My feet are underneath me swinging in this high oak tree, and let's say that maybe you and we could listen to stairway to heaven, in a field whose circumference is 37, three miles west from the corner seven eleven and or instead I'll reminisce over the past like it'll change anything in my future, realizing this I guess now I'll throw the first pitch. Don't think too deep see my mind it's a trick. It's very chill and very slick and won't allow me to join formations meaning no cliques. I'll just be a spiddyock with a straw hat, some wheat hanging out of the side of my mouth, blue overalls and a red checkered shirt. Tell these kids that my captain was KIRK. Tell them I grew up watching Big Bird and that when y'all grow up you all will remember Dora.

Never Came True

Sitting in the closet, hovering over mars and, I'm what you could say thankful in every way, that a girl like you would come one day. That I adore like a lazy donkey named Eyore and I like the idea of snoring next to you while our clothes are on le floor

Mean while on earth I was floating above the dirt on a dark dusk night, with heavy white clouds lingering in the sky. Driving through the desert on a streetcar named desire, flyer, higher than any of your deepest darkest desires. Your mind is for hire, and yet I'm on the swinging tire, dusty shoes and dirt on my cheek, thinking about going to the lake next week. Listening to Beck now I'm in a peaceful area where blue lights flutter the skies. I'm sorry; I made this playlist I think that you might like. It has the Beatles and Jimi Hendrix; oh you think that's tight?

That's when I saw the light in her eye, the one that lingers on and on without saying goodbye. I could see everything she was feeling, and they were oh so appealing. Like making your own meal down by the hill, above the chimney tops were we would play and dance and sing to orchestras as foreign as I could say. One day, I said, one day I'll buy you the universe. How quickly we are to converse things that seem appealing but somehow could never come true.

One After Another

Comfortably numb, I sit on my plumb. That's my behind like my past I constantly think about, dratz. I wish I could just run away with her and escape everything. Even though I'm not running away from anything bad, somehow I still feel sad. I feel like the other side of the moon that the sun doesn't reach, I feel like your first toy thrown at the bottom of the toy box. I don't feel wanted I just feel like I'm here. I'd rather spend my time with her and listen to Pink Floyd than go to a party where they are bumping Lloyd. I don't have an interest in money or having fancy things. I'm more concerned with my modern day flings and the way the sun lingers in the sky to the way that different birds take flight. Why does it take 350 degrees of heat to successfully bake a pie?

With all of these thoughts my mind goes back to her, I think too-too much. Maybe we should have some lunch, or maybe some cinnamon toast crunch. Or we can sit on my couch and play call of duty, play footsies, followed by us listening to some Bootsy Collins. As we holler hip hop hurray as we sit back and waste the rest of the day. I don't care; I'm the kind of person that thinks a perfect date is at the fair, comprised of dust and lights and a peaceful aurora the fills the atmosphere. With old music playing from musicians like Lou Reed; meanwhile a kid had fell in the dirt and scrapped his knee. I hate it when it gets too hot and I seem to attract the attention of bees, but it is part of life, without bees flowers wouldn't prosper. If you went any further with me, I probably wouldn't stop you. But now it is raining at my perfect fair date. If it's not too late to ask can I have another potential date, maybe dinner then afterwards we could skate? By this time if it was meant to be, well let's call it fate.

Unforgiveable Charity

Maybe clarity will come from me writing them down. Maybe it will come after the frown behind the clown's mound. Why does a clown frown? Is it because it's a grown man behind make up all caked up with lies behind a mask? Is it because he's unsure of the pleasure that he endured? Turning frowns upside down while yours remain. How obscured no way, the seducing of a man performed by a woman can leave you damaged. While trying to manage your emotion you took a walk to the ocean to step aside from the commotion. As the water floats onto your feet you grabbed a lawn chair and took a seat. Your baby girl went to the market and picked out your favorite meat, I can't beat it turkey ham for the man that's the plan, a meal I would steal for and give to the poor but I'd much rather purchase it from the store. –

By Suber

Lunch Break

Sometimes we are sad and our feelings take on full custody of our bodies. They hold us, like the kids on the bus in the movie Simon and Birch, when it swerved over the edge of the cliff into the freezing cold water. You ever just want to be somewhere else away from the world, where no such things as problems unfurl? There are no diseases and there's no unhealthy stress. The only things we have to worry about are how we should dress. We hot boxed the car that day, transporting us to this land where little animals carried trays with sprite in their hands. What you do in the dark will surely show in the light. It's never windy enough to go to the big field and fly a kite but every day is beautiful with you by my side.

There are so many things that I'd like to say to you. I foresee a connection unlike when I was a prepubescent adolescent. I think and therefore under my sole consent I would like to take you to an event, an event that takes place in your head, the location on my bed. Listening to sounds that travel through our ears to our brains. Too much music will make you insane. Take over your lanes; don't get pulled over by a cop on your journey though.

They no longer need to take down your license plates they just scan your car and a profile of you pops up like Face book. 40 years ago TV was the big medium now we have the Internet. No one foresaw the idea of cyber threats. No one really knows the hassle of still writing checks. But in a perfect world do you expect to be happy. I like the idea of being debt free with no taxes to pay, like the Indians before that dreadful day; like my little land of banned misfits.

It is night time now and the northern lights reflect the different colors onto the magical land. I wish I had a couple grand but that's another story. They had it so good back then. People could think and feel their emotions. They weren't just going through the motions. Let's be a band of hippies that just travel the world to explore, to adore, to rediscover the world.

I could write you something that would make you smile but would that really change the way your brain works. I want to be able to change people's thoughts by writing about what I am taught; what my brain perceives and conveys about the world. How to be happy and not be afraid of animals because we are all supposed to be in perfect harmony. Things that don't involve chase in my drink because alcohol diminishes your brain. It will eventually drive you insane, cutting down your brain power so that you can't think about what's really going on. I still don't want to talk on the mother freaking phone, but I will blast this Aerosmith until you dream on.

Where Art Thou?'

Where art thou'
In time of supper and chow
From the upbringing of the sun
To the nights that have yet to begun
From woods yet to be discovered
To fields failed before our yonder,
Upon them.
And in a whim, I'll rest tonight
and begin it all again.

The Way I Am

"Hello love," I said as I walked on by, hoping she remembers me long enough to increase her infatuation. All throughout my intricate thinking and keen observations, I noticed that she's breathtaking to say the least. As if I was in space with no astronaut suit or like the crazy fan off Eminem's song named Stan; driving into the water you are now holding your breath. Until your face is blue, in which next comes death. But oh no-no I just wanted to kick it with you. Eat these brownies and crank electric feel with you, but only when the sky isn't blue but when it is grey and gloomy and it has just rained and the ground is wet. The mud turns slippery and we have no regrets.

Or you can sit back and think about your regrets that soon shape the future for the next. Rambling on and on I took a step back and peered at you until our eyes made contact. Grabbed your hand and said please understand. The way I am is not by chance. So let's go to the fields so we can be as close to the moon as possible.

How dangerous it is to be frolicking about at night, let us wish that no vampires make their presence known, we might need garlic. Add in a wooden stake and a silver bullet for his werewolf counterpart, maybe a blanket, a lighter and some wood for our heat. A make shift range so that we can roast our meat. All within a shelter that aids in our relief, with a reply like "all here it goes" that comes next.

UckF

I was running down the steps and I tripped and broke the last step. In this case, I kept on falling down but it wasn't down at all. I fell up. I fell into a ceiling made of flowers. Somehow the world had switched sides. All of the trees were white and the grass was black. No one was poor; everyone had stacks, and beautiful houses that resembled your personality. If only this was an actual reality. Alcohol was illegal, marijuana vice versa; this place had it right, much-much better than Maryland. It was easy to find love because no one had problems they were all right in their minds. They were yet to be taken over by the rhythm and rhymes of the world, the ones that sound good, so you'll do it like a fool.

She showed me the world on a whole new light. The trees serve as lights in the dark. Leading a direct path to this heart shaped park. Enclosed by a gate in which only those with a pure soul could enter. The closer I got to the entrance the more and more it felt like the coldest winter.

The Journey Of A Droplet Of Water

I was watering the plants and I began to stare at the water hit the leaves of the plants and fall onto the ground. This made me ponder and I kept on pondering until I too became a single droplet of water falling from the leaf of my dreams. I'll attempt to find my way to the motherland, a stream which will in turn maybe lead into a sea or better yet an ocean where I'll get that good loving. There's more fish in the ocean than in the sea you see. So that's where I would like to be. To see potential in a candidate for my hospitality, okay I'm done talking about, well me.

A Thought Is Just A Thought

I stepped outside and realized that the world was more beautiful than I could ever have imagined. Let's not postpone though let's find some new magic's. This is for someone who has lost someone and it seems that there's no way, but there is I say. Life goes on, you must take what you learned and better yourself, not sit back burn yourself and sit in grief. Thinking about everything that could have been, think about the future moments that have yet to begin; although during the time you feel broken like an old ancient artifact chipped at its edges.

For instance, an old man walks through a dead forest in the middle of autumn with a straw hat and no destination but he has a devastating ability of persuasion. He just lost his ole' lady and he painstakingly has no clue on what to do. So therefore he walks everyday down this trail hoping something happens that'll make his life exciting again. And in a whim, as the days go by he notices that it's not so bad, his feelings of grief start to fade and he is no longer sad.

Things leave us, people leave us at some point, understand that nothing is forever and you'll be less affected by things that seem to haunt our memories. Like a spooky old house in the country with no windows. The steps creek and the trees lean up against it with its dead branches punching holes in the houses exterior. Holes take home in the faded white curtains. I'm almost certain someone beautiful used to live there. If you didn't know that's how I feel, like that house waiting for an inhabitant to reside. "Sleep with me by my bed side please," I said but not in the tone of me in need. It was more of a question expressed out of greed. You see once the house is tidied up it would be a lovely vintage house that a family could live in. Where they would fight and build memories that would shape their personalities. Naturally that's all that anyone could want, it seems like such a lovely picture but finding the right person to do so with is the daunting task. I just want go back in time when the days seemed to last longer than in my present age.

It Was Kind Of Like That

Flew in a plane from overseas and I landed in South Carolina, that's where I saw the trees. The deer's and the bees soon followed. But no one could tell me anything about the birds and the bees. That act was as natural as crawling on your knees. The trees would talk to me as a little kid. That'll go as far as your imagination will take you. You see, they talk but not with a voice, they talk with feelings, you either understand them or you don't. If you don't know but I'm sure you do they are responsible for healthy breathing. Some people have this ability to be one with their surroundings; it's quite outstanding, but rather lonesome. When you're out in the middle of nowhere you kind of have no choice but to learn to love life. Being fascinated with lightning bugs and how the trees seemed to hug when the sun no longer had a chuckle. A smell of sweet berries and old pine cones, shooting BB guns at old soda cans and bottles. If you'd just understand where you're at, love, and be at peace. Your life will accelerate at full throttle. Please put down those bottles, you don't need liquor to have fun; every disagreement doesn't have to involve a gun. However every morning will start with the rising of the sun, and it would be rather nice if you shared your last piece of gum. But uhm, I have dreams of everyone cooling it on the beach underneath a couple of palm trees as a bonfire illuminates the dusk inspired night sky. Listening to Bon Jovi and other cool cats that make you turn and twist your back. You know songs that make you dance a dance even if it's whack. It was kind of like that.

Κεεπ Ψουρ Προβλεμσ το Ψουρσελφ

On a yacht in my mind, the body of water trails slowly behind. Just relax a second take a deep breath and unwind. Be calm my friend; don't go insane, escape on the life train of this disastrous escapade, look back on it as you whittle away. Wondering what you did to waste those days; smoking purple haze, staring in a daze while eating a donut that's covered in glaze. We'll Converse about our mishaps in hopes of releasing our woes but honestly it'll only make things worse. Talking to you doesn't make the situation become at ease. It becomes harder like the last bit of ketchup in the 24 oz bottle that you're trying to squeeze. Please, I don't want to hear anymore, continue on your own path like Langston Hughes on the road less traveled. I'll travel down one road and come back later and take the other one; Feeling like I was kidnapped as a guerilla agent; a kid that's seven with a gun, raiding villages.

4th Of July

Sitting on the edge of the docks as the fireworks exploded in front of us. Making the lake glow different colors, I imagined that Jimi Hendrix was on stage behind us playing the star spangled banner. Sipping on some tea from 1962, on a peace blanket made from hippies out of naturally grown hemp. Don't be a skimp; sit back and zone out as you hear this guitar riff. Don't drop my spliff don't drop my spliff; Bob Marley would not like that not one bit. Every day the dock would call my name and ask me to bring my friend and we would sing our songs until we grew up and lost ourselves in the way of the world. Instead of having picnics at the dock, we ate dinner in every fancy restaurant that we could. No more sitting back watching movies all day long and then using my teeth to try and grab her thong. Listening to frank Sinatra like we ought to, but wait we have to formalize to society because in order for us to make a paycheck we have to follow the rules of someone else so that they too can get a paycheck. But what's a pay check to happiness? Why receive a reward for a day if it only brings a crappy mess. Why not live in a fort surrounded by life; plants and other wood inspired art creations. That'll keep you happy and increase your so called limitations; let's all switch to radical simplifications.

Synapses Of Earth

I woke up early this morning and watched the sun rise out of my window, wandering in my thoughts, hoping for revelations for my inner world. Right now being tired is killing me and I want to curl up in a ball or better yet start from space and set out on a journey like free-fall passing clouds that give knowledge as you pass through their core, learning secrets of the land, concoctions and quick sand. Once I got back to earth I began to feeble on its resources. It's rich and healthy landscapes, this was a beautiful place. But evil lurks every corner trying to tempt you. Making you decide between good and bad, happy or sad. I'll tell you of good fortunes that abide within all of us to be wealthy and fruit bearers with riches beyond belief in all good health. Without having to standout, use your skills, use your stealth. All good things must come to an end or a rest, to grow again or be reborn in one's own self.

Back In The Old Days

I kind of reminisce of cloudy days and their cousins called clouds and believe that as they rub their eyes, water falls down from the sky; On to a beautiful young lady that I'd like to kick it with, on a cool summer's night, sitting on the edge of the curb underneath of the pale orange street lights. I'll tell you of things that'll make your eyes glow bright, walking you home so that the nasties won't get you, like a Freddy Kruger or a Michael Myers. Leaving everything ablaze as we step through the fire and that's just the firewall in my brain because of how you made me feel.

Let's take a detour, the night is still early and your hair is starting to curl and I brought you to the park at five, around dark to talk to you about your dreams and aspirations to be. So that we could watch the sun set under the swing while our shoulders touched and it just felt right, do you know what I mean?

Wanting to kiss you underneath of the sunset as a dark orange glow filled with blue mist filled the sky and I could faintly start to see your face and your eyes. Then I would back away to ask you if you were still going to come outside another day. I never knew what you would say but you always said yes and so it always made my day.

Why don't you come back home with me and we could sleep for the rest of the early morning? A yes from her is what I was yearning. Her emotions her feelings is what I was learning. Trying to show her life through my eyes but not to rush anything because she was my sky and if you lose the sky all you'd see is the Milky Way and billions of stars, maybe an asteroid or a flying saucer. All this I thought of, as I saw her, one day walking the halls.

School, Mountains And A Desert

I pictured us sitting in a room lit up only by the blue ambience peering off of my laptop screen and TV, eating graham crackers and drinking fruit punch underneath of our specially built cover tipi. Castles made of sand played faintly in the background giving us a feeling of being on a beach early in the morning, next to a bonfire roasting beans in our baja hoodies.

The song has changed and so has my mood. I feel like I'm in a high school cafeteria eating lunch all alone, constantly checking my cellular phone in hopes of someone, something coming along; someone who matched the same rhythm of this song as I walked down the hall with my book bag hanging half way off of my arm. I'll look down at my feet but I can still see clearly in front of me so don't be alarmed. This is just life as a teenager in the 80's, with a ripped sweater and my favorite watch I've had since I was a baby, but the song has gone off now.

I'm now in a foggy autumn forest walking down a road in a grey suit being passed by an occasional motorcycle or coupe. The leaves fall from the trees towards the ground as if they were trying to add spices to a rather fancy soup and yet all I could think about was making it home to enjoy another bowl of fruit loops. But the song has now; you guessed it, changed again.

I'm walking in slow motion to your door step to tell you of how much that I was impressed by your witty humor and your ability to amuse yourself with the clarinet. But I turned around before I made it because I truly believed that you would never see me as your baby. Maybe a friend but everyone knows once you get stuck in the friend zone you're pretty much screwed beyond belief. That's when I saw a couple walking; holding hands and it gave me a sense of relief, which made my entire mood shift. So I turned around back towards your door because no sooner than five minutes later I started to believe. I started to conceive the idea of us being together in a house in the mountains, growing our food and letting our clothes dry on a clothing line in the front yard. You know, the white sheet flowing gracefully in wind. Where every once in a while we'd capture a bird, write a note on a little piece of paper and tie it to its claws to set it free in the hopes of it returning one day with a message from someone else.

The song however has changed once more. We are now in a desert with purple skies and a red ground that makes no sound. You can only hear the wind as it talks about its strange sightings and the shrieking howl of a pack of wild coyotes. "I'm sleepy are you ready to go to bed now?" Is what I asked her.

A Bad Love Note

Where is she; the solved cases to all of my mysteries; eyes of sunrise and a feeling of increased shivery. Sometimes I think about the thought of a dynasty but let's just keep that between you and me. Your aurora is ever enchanting like a princess with a story that's happily ever after. Like Jafar when he decided to go disobey his master. I should stop it there but I came back, to try and write you a story that's on a friend level is of an extremely rather high difficulty. What my mind perceives is not actual reality, so I'd picture a scene of us in a convertible driving in the desert, think about you in that scene while we listened to songs with no name, it adds to the effect.

Meanwhile this is all occurring in the delicacy of my brain. On a sudden juxtapose of thought we were crossing a north England bridge in the rain. The Dragons continually terrorize the neighborhoods, but many we have slain. We have earned more experience points, so we level up, I am now level 13.

The stoop kid won't hop down off of his stoop and Helga still won't tell Arnold how she truly feels. What's the big problem? I don't know but let's sit down in some type of comfortable position and solve them; Sharing candy bars out back, while the rest of the camp was inside eating their lunch. I brought you some cinnamon toast crunch. We laughed and decided to go back inside to this crappy butt lunch.

What To Call This

What if I just wrote this from my computer instead of my phone, and listened to songs by my favorite bands, while I thought about you. Not to consider my soda located on my desk that I have yet to drink, next to my chocolate bar and the Olympics playing in the background so low that the low playing music actually is louder than it. I'll think about you and our first kiss, underneath of the bridge, close to Christmas.

There was no snow on the ground but it felt like so. I really like those socks that you have with individual toes and your turtle neck sweater of the reindeer with the red lit nose. It really made you look beautiful, I suppose. Not to mention our adventures through the world, discovering the things that we so inherently enjoyed most. Like stirring up blue berry muffin mix until it was perfectly moist. Right now though, I'd like to just chill with you and play a couple of tunes. Maybe plug in some Lupe than next some blues, like muddy waters.

We used to be first up at bat for love like we were the starters, for love. Now it's rare that you have even an adept feeling for a hug. It's rather swell though; I'll just untangle my headphones and put this 3.5mm jack into its plug. Grooving to the sounds of my own music within, trying not to sin, high off life and a lack of oxygen.

Don't lose control, control your soul. Motives, feelings and desires are written all over your face. Only a few can discern these without a trace of this overwhelming ability. Somehow loving life keeps my humility. Keeps me sane, to see the beauty in total disdain and now I write to maintain total control over my brain. Like the government keeps hold of the mentally insane. In a cage because they are no longer able to benefit society, but we don't think, we've all lost our ability to see beyond things that are right in front of our face and so they have our sole propriety.

Shrimp

Eating shrimp fried rice and I'll go back onto the ship in which they were captured. Although Alice in wonderland is playing and it's on the part with the mad hatter. But I'll go on about that idea later down the ladder. I'd rather talk about being a shrimp in the ocean only to be taken from your home next to a shore that's close to being eroded. It was our hangout spot, down by the old sunken ship, that's where shrimpette and I first touched our lips. That's where I started writing this script. Let us go to the seaweed forest and sneak into the shark's houses and taste a fraction of each of their porridge. Wait, wait, wait, that's not the right story.

Love Is An Illusion That You Must Learn To Live With

Sitting out there, I read you a book as I noticed you carelessly playing in your hair. You were lovely, in fact, I would have loved to call you my honey, but I cringed at the thought of being attacked by a bear. These writings I write for you I hope someday will make us some money. If so, I'll buy a guitar and play musical compositions for you every day until your heart and ears become one in the same. I promise I'll stick with you if the so called two evils trot towards my way; they're called fortune and fame. I'll remember how you sat with me and ate your lunch so lovely on the blanket next to me not dropping a single crumb as I wrote on parchment paper underneath of the shade that was ever changing at a rapid pace. Keeping up with my pencil line after line, one minute it was 12, the next a quarter after nine. Help me gather my things and lets go inside, tomorrow is a new story; one hell of a minds ride.

The Woods, After It Has Snowed. I Have No Place To Go.

This is the story of Oswald In the middle of the forgotten forest during winter's harsh freezing cold conditions. Setting flags down so that I'd know if I was going in complete circles, marveling at the snow falling in perfect cubicles, landing on the ground taking up all of earth's particles. So I'll step with my left foot and make a crunch, next comes my right foot as my stomach begins to growl. As I hear a soothing sound of a hoot from an old wise owl that could tell you a different story pertaining to the exact square inch of the mile. But it's rather cold now, too cold to function, too cold to keep on chugging down the trail in hopes of getting out of this winter of a hell. I notice a little spot where I could set up camp, but I'll need to start a fire so I proceed to find firewood that's not damp. In the middle of winter, that seemed to be a daunting task all in itself. Maybe a helicopter will pass and notice the smoke rising above the trees. Thinking about how soldiers used to communicate in old battles actually took my mind off of all of the sounds I heard, the rattles. A brush and a crunch, my nerves were all in bunches, not to mention I still haven't had my lunch yet. Trying to stay warm I'll huddle next to the fire as the flames gently raise the temperature in the spaces surrounding. I peered out and saw beautiful backdrops of white trees and tall mountains. It kept me warm on the inside like two hand-warmers next to my heart. This was art, and I was in the painting being drawn by an artist while it was snowing.

Free From TV, Welcomed By the Trees

Technology has us captured like a cage in a beast. Who's only fed with ignorance placed on the TV, soon followed by nano-bots that inhabit your brain and alter your speech, leaving us with problems pertaining to protecting our free speech.

Do you know what's going on in the world, our world, the world in which you partake your living upon? No, and so let us sit up on this stone gated bridge and practice singing our gracious swan song for when the time arises. Floating down the stream underneath of the moonlight, listening to crickets and other animals that make you say "what was that?" Tilting my hat so that I could peer out in front of me, staring at the stream as the ripples jilted off into the distance; where our eyes would eventually meet.

I must ask, "Do you like hotdogs and beans?" it's about all that I have left to eat. This was before technology, before the TV. I didn't get her number; we exchanged love, underneath of the willow tree. Of course I asked her questions like "what dreams inhabit thee?" She responded with an answer filled with glee, a feeling which even put a smile upon the willow tree. Let's gather some essentials and take camp by the stream. I'll tell you some stories that'll make you laugh and then scream. Like some little kids in a pair of overall jeans.

That made you laugh so I see that I can seal the seam that seems to be splitting like a broken heart straight down the middle. Jingle-Jeimer, get up let's do a little jig, I'll play you some music glowing from my fiddle and we can sit by the stream for the rest of the night laughing as we toss more wood into the fire. As nature soon becomes our natural choir.

Simplicity Will Save Us All

All I want is a bit of happiness, some joy and a place to live. Where I'd blast the spinners because whenever you call me I'll surely be there, I'll surely be around. Maybe somewhere outside taking it all in, trying to meditate, trying not to sin. So that I'll continue to live problem free you see with God you actually win. But dwell on that and notice how well placed everything is, two hours away and it's like I arrived on another planet. With a spaceship made out of dirt so that I can plant trees in order to receive a bit of oxygen. I don't need a suit I just need this spaceship and maybe a couple pieces of wood too.

Don't ask how the electricity works just know that it did and I built it in Central Park in New York, a little bit after four, before the old man dropped his keys, before opening his store. As the lady walked in after him shortly to purchase his products in which case she didn't really need them but that's a different subject.

You know, I was just thinking. What if everyone turned off the TV cut off their internet and turned in their phones. Let's go back to building our own homes, going outside real early and not returning to the early morning, making friends with everyone along your journey. Reading books and learning how to do all types of trades that our world was founded upon. Let's all get together and play a game of tag, instead of talking about how the next person has no swag. Dress how you want who cares what the next person thinks, just let them be mad. Mad that you're further progressed in your mind, passed the level that society has set for everyone. I say in everything you do, look for the good of it, make it enjoyable, and make it fun.

On Land Or On Sea, I Still Think About Thee

Rowing the ocean blue with food for ten days and a total of seven crew members, I'm so glad that we didn't decide to do this in December when the wind is a bitter cold and the waters are freezing. It'll make you sneeze I tell you and someone will have to bless your highness or be forever cursed by Davey Jones locker.

While sailing, all I could think about was being back on dry land, maybe playing soccer or anything that would make me sane. All I see are seagulls, rocks and other things that'll make you just want to slip in your chair and gently start to pace back and forth. "Where are we headed sir," well young lad we are headed north.

More flashbacks occur like eating sunflower seeds back on my porch. While my beautiful neighbor swung on her swing set underneath of the oak tree. Oh if I made it back I would confess my love to her and tell her how it should be; me and her going to the old diner and having a sundae for two, with two straws coming out of each end. As I choose an Elvis song for five cents, so I want to know if I can have this dance underneath of my tent tonight.

A storm is now brewing and I came out of my daydream because a day dream is never what it seems. I'll have to come back to reality, so what does it all mean? I don't know but the waves sure were getting mean making me sea sick and dizzy. So I guess I'll throw up on the side of the boat and keep it moving, even though my mouth felt a little fizzy. The only thing keeping me steadily going were my thoughts of her in the morning lasting throughout the evening.

Μεδιτατινγ Αλονγ

As I am sitting Indian style in the middle of the grass, meditating on life and everything that I see that I consider to be trife, I wonder why people would want that in their life. But you know I could show you something grander than just fancy things. I'll take you to places where there are old rusty swings that creak as the wind pushes up against it. Right there behind the old wooden house.

But enough of a flashback that never happened let us think about life in all of its subject matter. You aren't bigger than the universe, no decision you make will change anything for better or for worse. But please oh please listen to this song with me please. I have to test your soul see how truly one you are with yourself. Or are you conformed to societies views because you don't know anything else. I bet you didn't know with faith you could move mountains to the sea side, but look at us we sin everyday down by the high tide. Where we laid there and talked about life until I began to get that feeling right above my thigh.

When I kiss you, close your eyes. I heard the experience is better than going to the movies to see The Dark Knight at night, with a bad brains beanie and no flashlight. Enough, I've had it up to here, things should change but our minds have been too rearranged. They're deranged and so complicated like a rubix cube with 10 different faces, 10 colors and 10 different pronunciations. So as I realize things about this world that I want to refrain from. I'll water the plants every other day and be stuck on nature and all of its fixations.

A Girl to Greed

Oh how art thou so beautiful and yet your mind is not the same so readily. When a chance presents itself why let it waste but then I began to think about you not being able to see on the same level as I. So I'll sit outside and write about how I could have been of so much help and now I'm tossed to the side like an old tied up rope. I'm not taking it there that's a story in itself. So follow me down the steps and I'll show you to this magical shelf.

If you didn't notice, we'll keep walking forever because the magical shelf, well that's a story in itself. See this shelf I speak of is nowhere to be found it's inside all of us whether skinny or rather round. It's our imagination and I'll tell you, it is a wonderful creation. A simple thought and henceforth comes a world of inspiration.

Into the living room now and I'll tell you of tonight's preparations. Bring me some tea, a notebook and three different females giving me their attention and I'll teach you of the demise of all three. In the end you receive none of thee, but a seldom lesson of how to be more trustworthy. I'll stop that story now, because that won't be me. When you use what you are taught in a lesson in life you grow in other ways that won't affect your body. Instead it'll keep you looking young and completely stress free. Just allow your mind to settle real deep. Think about everything pertaining to your problem and see that it is not truly as bad as your emotions made it to seem. That riding a bike, thinking positively about life makes you healthier and happy all of the time. Doing a good deed for a person in need seeps its return, open your eyes and see. Then will you start to achieve a greater wealth. The bad is not of this world so don't focus on that, because who are you following if it is nothing. You are following nothing and therefore miss what's good, right in front of your face.

Now, I think it's time we go to the basement. You see this is where your memories make their statements like bill collectors if you miss a couple of payments. Your job is to make my life worse by asking for a thing of greed which everyone seeks. Therefore creating gluttony and this will lead to more and more greed. Now look, one is the King and the other is looking for food on the side of a street.

Robin owes Tom money 100 times over; Tom is nice enough to let Robin off debt free and if everyone was this nice life would be so easy. But Robin sees a man that owes him money and releases all hell onto his debtor, not seeing that he was just blessed. He was an all around mess and word spread to Tom; he returned to Robin and asked "why haven't you given favor to this man like I had on you?" "Now pay me back the fines that are due", for Robin did not see that he was blessed and instead felt greed, so that he could bathe in the riches of mere coins. A learnt life lesson in which I read from the book of life, okay now you may gently fall asleep.

Sitting Under A Tree In The Backyard

Thick blue and white socks keep my feet warm as I sneak into the outside world in hopes of being a book worm. Destroying my television and all other electrical devices, I'll communicate through telekinetic energies and the wind as I whisper back into it as it passes me by. Hoping it'll reach the ear of someone in need. But for now I'll keep quiet and buy two large sweet teas.

Back to my little hideaway in a cave, lit up by two bug lanterns that creates a foggy haze. Making the end look as close as the beginning and yet it has depth that would make you think that it's never ending. Okay, so while I go on my E-break and become like an animal in nature. Turn to the next page.

What Used To Be A Love

Lying in the grass with my beautiful love, I call her my best friend because all in all she's a dove. Our secret spot is by the pond it's full of algae and full of Lard. The animals that reside in the territory make funny noises sometimes we turn them into stories. They appear to get closer the less you think about them but I think it's just a couple of frogs singing to the moonlight on top of a log.

When 12 o' clock strolls around, that is when it starts to turn foggy. That's when we'll skip rocks with fruit snacks and watch them start to turn soggy. Or lie back down and watch the stars as I pull the blanket back over us. Cuddling for warmth especially since the sun no longer can fuss, and when you're outside at night it gets a little chilly. That's why I came prepared and I stopped by Wendy's for their 99 cent chili. I felt like at sometime while we were laying there some kid that was named Billy, would walk by and start to snicker. I'd push him in the pond and think of something clever like, snicker on that, hungry why wait. Besides that point I think someone's coming. I heard a gate lift up, so we began to scat, got the hell up out of there, straight like that.

Now I'm carrying you on my back, trying to take you back to my place. I have some unfinished business with you and oh so little time to waste. So let me turn on some music that gets you into the mood and I'll kiss you underneath the black light until you're frozen and hungry for some food. Somehow a little Wayne song came on from the mix tape no ceilings and everything was ruined but I already started the downfall of diminishing my feelings.

A Road In Comparison With Your Soul

Sitting in a room being flooded by the light of a dying sun, somewhere in this span of time I began to run, and I kept on running down this street which never ended. Bushes and flowers grew alongside of the road but never on it. Making sure my path was always clear before me. On the outskirts of the road there were old houses and lots of trash. None of which ever touched the street. I never had to avoid anything that could potentially lead to a crash. This road was perfect and yet if I strayed I would end up in the vast wasteland that would in turn lead me nowhere. So I'll keep following the road until it takes me somewhere, somewhere full of riches and glory and knowledge beyond comprehension to the average being.

So for now I'll let you see only a little bit of the wisdom stored inside of me through my writings. But I'll always be in the shadows hiding looking and abiding. Binding those things that try to come before me, now where were we?

I want to evoke feelings in you that travel through your body and out of your brain. I guess you could say that I was a little out there but to me I just call it knowing your subconscious. That pretty much will keep you honest, and you'll never ever think about breaking another pinky promise.

Sleep

Let me see, let me see, I could think of a million and one things, but would that make you an ultimate being. Somehow tranquility makes you one with your inner world. I'll try to explain so listen up. Staring at the sky as the sun starts to drop, your body starts to change and then what? You leave your body and your problems are no longer weighing you down. It's like driving through town with your windows down and your music blasting, even if winds were hitting you that were as cold as Aspen. Once you leave your body you become like the sky or the waves depending on where you are. Then you are life, flowing and growing. A tree has no stress unlike grass when I'm going over it with my lawn mower. And so it grows for years and years and years just giving life to us humans. But let's cut it down instead so that we can create amusement. Maybe a house or a store with a basement and four floors which mean even more trees need to be cut down for all of the doors. In which I'll tap my foot on to check how sturdy it is, as I wish underneath of the stars like a little kid staring out his window only to see one go flying by. Just ask why, and your mind will die, only to come back to life stronger than ever. Now if only I could decide what I want to wear in this unpredictable weather.

I Thought That We Would Run Away Together

Come on let's escape this hell hole of a place, where no good has ever come. Well at least not in good haste. I refuse to waste any more time with you, I'll be back over when the sun begins to drop and shadows over take the land like an army from the southern lands. Bring some of your books, clothes and maybe an apple or two. I'll tell you why you'll need those things if you promise me you'll never be blue. I'll keep you happy and your mind will be free from all of the evils that could potentially haunt thee. It's time for me to leave I will be sitting in the tree above your window pane at the time I designated earlier.

Bye I said with a wave of my hand and a head nod. As I dropped down from the tree my foot slipped from underneath me and I slipped on a row of sod. Still smiling because later on my heart would be filled with the presence of this goddess, of course she didn't see my happiness, I remained upmost modest. When in all honesty, she made me feel like some water being boiled on an open range awaiting its tea bag to give it a certain taste.

My day dreams concluded as the sun did its job and dropped below the skies. At this time I would usually lay my head down as my eye lids closed in on one another, but I had a mission that would take us to the yonder. We would get out of this place and better yet not leave a trace. I waited and waited and paced hence forth and back again two times, then four times and I began to become worried. Like a boy who waited patiently for his mother to buy him a toy. Only to be denied at the register because it was more than she had expected. This couldn't be happening to me, I guess all the time she had alone, left her to think and now I was being rejected, like water going down a stopped up sink. I just blinked profusely, trying to indulge in my head what could have possibly gone wrong. Maybe it was something I said? So I just walked on home stopping by the market to pick up a loaf of bread.

What Are The Motives?

You were a jewel to me like the motive of a group of people trying to set their life right by robbing a bank that was entirely too wealthy. Thinking thoughts like that and you'd never expect them to be of good health. But they robbed this bank and took the jewel only to be faced with moral conflicts that coincide with the natural balance of things. Like a swing set being pushed by the unforeseen force of the wind, or maybe there's invisible people sitting down meddling. Who's to keep this jewel and who could sell it? And how were these hopeless people going to avoid being sent to jail. Who knows?

As I check my mail box on this phone that's given me the rightful duty of writing these notes, while I sit outside underneath of a trifecta of trees in the back. Wondering why everyone I keep running into turns out to be in fact whack. Whack whack-whack, like that, like that mole game you play with your girlfriend at the fair, I can't answer that question so instead I'll relapse and get some fresh air; hold onto this despair and collapse onto a bed of mulch being surrounded by plants of different kinds, all the plants blending in together with no egos trying to take flight. Lest they be hijacked by insects crashing into the ground splitting off at its esteem forming roots. All of this is quite delightful I thought to myself as I quietly mesmerized about life inside of my head. Wishing you could feel the same things I felt like listening to music notes with dual head buds and a two liter bottle of water right out of the factory polluting the air, letting us inhale oxygen that's less than satisfactory. I'm kind of mad now so let me go inside of my head and fight this mad kid so that he can't bully my other helpless emotions.

Story Time

Shhh, shhh grandpa is about to start his story; somehow it strangles your attention forcing you to witness its visions. One sentence, one scene and yet a picture is worth a thousand words, a scene more like ten million. Still sitting Indian style, with both my hands placed firmly on my cheeks, hearing a snap crackle and pop from the fireplace that's giving off such a soothing heat. We heard the creaking of his rocking chair and listened to a story that travels deeper and deeper, down the trail and alongside the creek.

My hands had slipped off my cheek and I fell forward. Trying to be humble trying to be meek, I picked myself up and carefully retook my seat. What happened in the story next I have yet to know. Grandpa's chair had stopped rocking and he was sound asleep. Maybe next time I'll know what happens when the boy crosses the creek, I'll imagine I am him as I walk swiftly across the street; in tune with my imagination as if someone was drawing my life like a famous cartoon.

Let's just say that same day I took a journey trek to the moon but I had only crept up to my room, to go peacefully asleep until the following day's noon.

Camping Trip
In Our Mind's

She beautifully glanced towards me and to my delight, I was once afraid of heights and now I'll travel with you by night. To our little camp located in a random location in the woods. We'd meet up to justify our behavior during the day, mentoring each other so that we both could remain sane. Lovely night isn't it, I said to her to initiate conversation.

We would lay on our backs, looking peacefully at the sky, I tried to just catch a single glimpse of her out the corners of my eyes, peering through the tree branches that gave an outlining of the sky. It was drawn comparable to a cartoon, being outlined by some guy. Peace is all that we had to seek and it is all that we so coherently received. Until time gave way and our eyes began to stray. Into the back of our heads as our eye lids started to enclose the world around us. To be awoken at the earliest of times the next day by a metro transit bus. Our fire had gone out and so did all of our billions of friends in the sky. Too soon, and now we must rendezvous at another time. Set the date and bring your most valuable chest; your mind.

Turn Off The Media, Turn On Your Mind

Casually we fall back into the frame work of our existence, futile to new beginnings our lives are in cages, swinging from a rope in some dry forgotten cave. Little do we know of the world outside of this cave because our minds have only been told of the brown rock surrounding us. Not of nature's most brilliant fortress which doesn't include cars and raggedy air polluting buses. Everyone's inhaling the fumes while constantly eating an insatiable amount of fast food. Only to be given heart problems that'll make our hearts turn blue. Not like the sky but like after you've been holding your breath for about three minutes and your brain starts to die off because of the lack of oxygen in it, that kind of blue.

Are we all a little blue already. With a banjo, a harmonica and a band with deep voiced musicians who play chords that make you think about their depressing inhibitions. Yet music seems to describe the state of the world, right now we're all about cars, clothes and hoes; our music has lost purpose and with that goes its soul. But music isn't the only thing that shapes the minds mould. Television is most whole heartedly responsible for what the people are told. So it's never on anymore because I don't want to be told a vision, I'd rather create my own, through reading and knowledge seeking long for told and hidden by the creation of technology in our threshold.

Watching Television for me has now been replaced with reading and writing and being poetic about what color the sky is. The first few days and I am at most the least excited, right now I'll sit all day and not even have urges to fight it. My mind is free and the rest shall flow freely within this world strictly confined by what's portrayed in the media.

Grown Ups

Stuck in this vortex of space I call my wonderful mind. I wonder to myself if you'd like to travel through its depths and discover mysteries about me that'll loosen chains around yours. Comforting as it may seem, every night that I lay my head upon my pillow, it is you that inhabit my dreams. I travel through time and space in an unknown place trying to clear my thoughts so that I could present them to you in a timely manner. That's when you'd get that feeling that you have when you have a 30 minute presentation that you've so desperately been waiting for, only to mess up and realize that life still goes on. Although these butterflies in my stomach have now grown fond of their new home; as if you were a droplet of kryptonite in my bloodstream. Heading down the road straight for the inner city towards my cardiac muscle known as a heart, passing kids doing kick flips on skateboards yelling "eat my shorts" as if there idol was that kid name Bart.

To some it all up, you're a porcelain cup in a wooden forest, sticking out like such and so beautifully woven. Thinking ahead, waking up early mornings to you pulling food out of the oven. While the news played louder than usual so that we could catch what they were saying even if we weren't paying attention. It's not like we had to rush or anything, we made our lives full by doing what we enjoyed doing the most. Bringing our imagination and intelligence together to crack open the hard deals of life, that you don't really have to go through. Avoiding mishaps by reading the paraphrases when taking a book and turning it on its back, I tell you, I tell you life is as good as you make it and we made is just that.

La, La Land

Indulge, indulge, indulge, I need some inspiration but it seems to be hidden at this very hour. So I'll take you on a random journey, deficient of a firewall to keep the thoughts in a sane manner.

We fell back off of the bed and we kept falling until we were inside of a black whole filled with your dreams and memories. This isn't my first time here but this is all new to you and so I held your hand as we became closer to the end, turn up straight so that you'll land on your feet. Too late and we hit with a thump, the kind that'll make your tush hurt for the rest of the night. I call this black land because everything is dark but everything is comparable to earth with no inhabitants. Just me, you and whoever else we would like to consider as constituents, to pay the rent to reside in our dual imagination land. The sea is sand and the sand is sea so which is which I have no idea. Although they still perform the same functions, it was confusing to see, like being a little kid trying to learn how to properly use conjunctions.

Let's continue through the darkness, which we can vividly see in, so is it really dark or a term that we just haven't reasoned out with yet. The trees danced with the wind as if they were at the last ball, before fall and their demise would soon start to arise. They would change colors and be kicked off of their branches to fall towards the ground, sky diving with no parachute gently like a balloon with no helium. Orange now over took our world, our imaginations liked the idea so much it was out of our control. The bodies of water tasted like sprite with a little bit more lemon than an even amount of lime. Yet it was natural and so we drank until our bodies gave way and screamed "ENOUGH," at the top of their lungs. They were bodies, so they could do that.

I filled up my canteen for later on because that sprite was more than just a delight. It was light wherever we had gone. Through the hills of ravishing rapids and the trails of the forgotten beards, we lost track of time and it was about close to that time. Where we'd wake up and be kicked out of our minds. I heard a faint noise and it rapidly got louder, only briefly after did I awake next to a tree staring at a couple of stratus clouds slowly passing by.

All Aboard

There is knowledge to be bestowed upon all of us, read a book as we sincerely pay our homage. Take a journey to release your body of these chemicals that deteriorate our age, and improvements will start to concur that allow you to be able to skate, when you are 80 years old without the help of Medicaid.

You are able to run through the fields, still healthy from the days when you were a hippy tripping out on life in the still of the night. Peacefully mellowing out underneath of the pale moonlight, not like a drifter though but like on a midnight train to Georgia, foot hanging out of the side of the stock cart, three feet above the gravel. Constantly staring out into the fields while traveling 25 miles per hour traveling the land trying to make money from your make shift band. In which you brought your instruments from thrift stores in Southern Maryland.

Gninrom

Gninrom backwards is Morning as I tip my hat to you, wave and say how are you? Fine you say; me too. Don't know you but I'd like to get to know ya. Cool around in the pool splashing in the cash keeping her away from these tools. Fools that is, with no intentions but to fuck for free, not even a buck, not even a walk in the park to feed the ducks. Her shit say fuck what have I done this shell sucks, outer shell gorgeous, inner soul scorching like a blazing forest. Scared for life making moves like she rolling dice chancing it, pick a card any card the magician says jumping on some kegs with excitement. This guy is drunk she thinks and he winks with the card in his hand while he squirts his mist fan and out drawn from his hand was life. Gave her chance to dance in the heavens and not be so trife but to enjoy life for a healthier price. She was so siced that this blessing came from the heavens, blessed number seven.

By Suber

Beautiful Spirit

Only when I'm sad can I tap into these powers bestowed upon me. Crazily my thoughts are clear and I feel the effects of weed, without the smoke and a cough without the choke. It's okay it's just the mountain air clearing my mind allowing me to digress upon my thoughts. Leading me to think about her and how we were so beautifully matched in the heavens. My soul yearns for hers and hers for mine and yet she is blinded by sunlight without a pair of sunglasses to make her look fly. So our feelings shall die like a tree during winters harsh cold conditions. Only to be brought back to life at another season, I say this as if it was a premonition.

Two points mapped in the universe will touch if they are profoundly meant too and so I hang my hat up on the wall and throw my jacket on the back of this old wooden chair, running my hands through my hair hoping to feel relief from my now hurting heartbeat. I'll stare at the endless roads as I peer at both directions before crossing the street. Faintly in the background right behind an enormous cloud, lies a beautiful mountain peak, not close to the resemblance of the beauty I see in thee, somewhat comparable to a chill day frolicking in the southern fields on a warm sunny evening.

There was a tree that stood tall In the middle of the field that's where I want you to meet me at whenever you feel lonely or get ill. Or if your thoughts start to get a hold of you and you can't release your thoughts grasp. There in the middle of the tree stood our initials with a heart enclosed around it. I presume our love is in comparison to a tree that hasn't died in ages, one who stuck it out through thick and thin, through the hottest of summers, including winters harsh conditions.

Let's stop with all of our pointless reminiscing if you feel that you must forget me because you don't deserve me, than go. Your heart has such a great stronghold in which the purest of hearts cannot enter and so I sit outside your heart and talk to you from the window instead, wishing, hoping that I could climb up to your bed but I can't because your thoughts came out side and kicked me from in front of your breathtaking beauty for loitering.

So I wander back into the forest of your mind, not forgotten, just out of plain sight. I'll come back in due time and I'll spark your interests, but if you don't think you're ready I still can never truly rest. I've traveled the land and I've never seen such a beautiful fortress of a heart such as yours in which I desire. Yet at the top of the love scale it declines until my eyes turn into fire, from your decisions that make the least sense.

Can you let down your draw bridge and let me sit on one of your veins. The closer I get the more you'll back away in disdain. So I'll step further in hopes that you'll place one foot ahead of the other instead of backwards but all of my words just make you feel awkward.

I'm banished from your heart once again with my picture hanging on your hearts castle walls, saying do not let this man on our premises. Yet you know that you'd rather have me be the king of your castle. Yet you'll allow the staff to do as they please. Hoping to just forget about me and that makes no sense. I'll come back every night when the moon is at half crescent, right outside your window. If the time permits itself let me up, if not, I'll be back. I'll travel the woods alone if I can't have your majesty's affection in recollection with your hearts satisfaction and your minds dedication, all in perfect synchrony. Not blind by society or what others may think. Just come outside your heart and see from my point of view and in one blink you'll see that I'm your future.

She still just stares at me from her window until the guards come kick me from out front until tomorrow.

The End

Notes

Notes

Made in the
USA
Middletown, DE

75522560R00085